Soul Sisters

Soul Sisters

The special relationship of girlfriends.

Cheryl Saban PhD

Friendship is a treasured gift, and every time I talk with you I feel as if I'm getting richer and richer.

Friendship is a treasured gift, and every time I talk with you I feel as if I'm getting richer and richer.

UNKNOWN

LONDON • NEW YORK

Senior designer Toni Kay
Commissioning editor Annabel Morgan
Picture research Christina Borsi
Head of production Patricia Harrington
Art director Leslie Harrington
Editorial director Julia Charles

First published in 2013 by
Ryland Peters & Small
20–21 Jockey's Fields
London WC1R 4BW
and
519 Broadway, Fifth Floor
New York, NY 10012
www.rylandpeters.com

ISBN 978-1-84975-355-5

Printed and bound in China.

A CIP record for this book is
available from the British Library.

Contents

Introduction

Girlfriends. The cherished, unique bond that women share binds many of us together heart and soul. I've heard many of my friends say, *"I don't know what I'd do without my girlfriends...I'm not sure I could get through my days without them."* Those are strong words, and the sentiment behind them runs deep. Girlfriend units are often so close-knit that they become akin to a sisterhood.

Imagine some of the most significant moments in your life and the people you've chosen to be by your side to share them, and I'll bet a cherished girlfriend pops into your mind. You may have created a network—a 'broad squad', as one of my friends calls her cherished buddies. There's a good chance many of these girls and women are among those in the cheerleading section of your life when you need them most. Why is that? Because your girlfriends make you feel good. They understand you. They have your back. Ever since you were young, you sought out girls that you liked, and made an effort to befriend them. And though there may be squabbles, ups and downs, and the occasional serious, irreconcilable break up, during the course of your life, you'll have found some girlfriends that have held fast. These women are your support group.

Some of those girls became short-term friends, and others last throughout your life. But whatever the case, you and I know that girlfriend soul-sisters are almost as important to us as our primary relationships are (some would say *more* important) and, like treasures, they are worthy of special care and attention.

Girlfriends help shape who we are, and they listen, support and commiserate with us as we flesh out who we want to become. So, whether you're giggling like schoolgirls over tea for two, or bitching and complaining like adolescents over witches brew, make sure you seek out, and treasure your girlfriends. It's good for you!

Settle back and enjoy. This little book is a tribute to you. Cheers, kudos, bravo, yahoo, thank you and, most of all, love to female friends and soul sisters everywhere.

*Friendship is a single soul
dwelling in two bodies.*

ARISTOTLE

Soul Sisters

Where we met, What we share, What keeps us together

Secrets, *sharing*, laughing, crying, understanding, husbands, emotions, psychology, knitting, travel, *care-giving*, death of a loved one, *yoga*, philanthropy, tea and biscuits, hiking, *parents*, skiing, siblings, lunches, *heartache*, baby showers, boyfriends, children, cake, a love of chocolate, motherhood, cooking, a tragedy, *careers*, movies, telephone conversations, texts, occasional letters, summer camp, *graduation*, working together, email, dance class, girl scouts, camp-fire girls, church, paddle-boarding, *comfort*, surfing, politics, travel, long walks, *spiritual experiences*, pole dancing, Pilates, card games, birth of a child, dessert, holding hands, hugs, *a knowing glance*, bridal showers, *everything*, pure friendship, a true, abiding kind of love...hard to describe in words... you have to feel it...you just know!

Socializing and Connecting

Make time

Girlfriend time is therapeutic. It can actually
improve your health, and help you live better.

We share secrets with our girlfriends, we laugh with our girlfriends,
and we cry with our girlfriends. We might even have the occasional
argument with our girlfriends—hey, we're only human! But when we
calm down and make up, we often become even closer afterwards.

We women bare our souls, share our emotions, and talk about the intimate details of our lives with our girlfriends. We're surprisingly willing to share specifics that even our husbands and relatives don't know. Perhaps it's because we feel safe with girlfriends in ways that we can't always articulate. They are the ones we turn to when we need to vent about our relationships, complain about our kids, and cry about our disappointments, because we know they'll understand. Girlfriends are our cohorts, confidantes, role models, and support system. They understand our mood swings, and let us yammer on about the same gnarly subject that has us troubled until we get it out of our system… something the men in our lives may not be capable of doing.

Girl buddies help us moderate stress and lessen the sorrows that inevitably occur during our life journeys. A group of girlfriends is a commune we build among ourselves—a modern-day version of the Biblical red tent. We need it—our own special place and time.

Let us be grateful to people who make us happy, they are the charming gardeners who make our souls blossom.

MARCEL PROUST

"The girlfriends I had were girls I met after I got married. We started a canasta group, and there were eight of us, all good friends. Two of us were pregnant at the same time. We were always there for each other. We had pot-luck dinners at each other's houses, and we babysat each other's kids so we'd get a chance to go out once in a while. The older you get, the more you appreciate your friends, because now some of them are gone. But I still remember those that are gone, and all the good times we had together." *Betty*

"Girlfriends are my extended family…the family I have chosen! They are reliable, caring, fun, consistently there for me, and for their other friends too. I could not live without them." *Martha*

Girlfriends are a great support network

Share what you know. Be trustworthy with one another
and give encouragement.

Go on an adventure together

Take a vacation, a dance class, pottery lessons, or learn to play poker.
Let your little girl out to play, and have fun. It's never too late
to be young at heart with your girlfriends.

"There doesn't seem to be an age limit on having fun with girlfriends.
When we get a chance to be together for a ski or yoga trip—which is rare,
because of kids, and careers, and husbands and homes and board meetings,
and all the other responsibilities of our busy lives—we can still laugh like
schoolgirls. Our hearts are light, and we let ourselves go. Love bounces
around like light, and there is a special kind of warmth and glow around
us that just beams—lightens us. This light and warmth lasts a long time.
We can all draw from the fountain of youthfulness of a trip like that
for years, for a lifetime, if need be. Girlfriend bonding time is like
breathing giggle gas. It makes you smile." *Lynn*

"I was once invited to a rather unique 'girls' dinner party. My friend, the hostess, was a little secretive about the reason for the party, but she did mention that it was going to be a little bit naughty, but fun. Little did I know! We had margaritas first, then gathered around a table with an expert who brought in a whole display of sex toys and showed us how to use them! We all got a chance to show off our various skills, and we laughed and laughed until we cried. It was hilarious. We had the best time together and, of course, we vowed to keep the details confidential. We'll never reveal who had the best—um—skill at certain activities, but we were proud to discover that all of us girlfriends had our tricks, and though we were a range of ages, that didn't seem to matter. Oh, how we laughed. We could only imagine what our men would have given to be a fly on the wall that night! It was a memorable evening—one that this group of girlfriends will long remember!" *anonymous*

Giggle like schoolgirls, share secrets, laugh and be silly

The pure enjoyment of being with a friend will brighten and lighten your day.

Be a good listener

Pay attention, and actually focus on what your girlfriend is saying.
It's not your job to fix your girlfriend's problems, but try to listen
attentively, respectfully, and without judgment, so she
can feel heard, supported, and validated.

"I have some girlfriends that I call my 'crew,' and we work on similar projects in the same field. On one particular occasion, when I began facilitating a committee, it didn't go so well—in fact, it fell apart, and at the end, I felt dejected. I shared my experience and disappointment with my crew. They listened and then kindly, yet honestly, told me that I 'blew it,' and that's why I felt so bad. They went on to give me constructive criticism about how to improve for the next meeting. They gave it to me straight, and I took it all in my stride. I rocked the next meeting. My 'crew' and I have each other's backs—we're there for each other. We help each other when we fall, and celebrate each other's triumphs." *Debbie*

It's not so much our friends' help that helps us, as the confidence of their help.

EPICURUS

"Don't walk in front of me, I may not follow. Don't walk behind me, I may not lead. Walk beside me, and just be my friend. Girlfriends are as important as the air we breathe." *Danica*

"My heart races when I think about my girlfriends. I can't wait to see them, and I feel that we are invincible when we're together. I couldn't live my life without mine…it's true love. That's what soul sisters are all about. My soul sisters helped me have my son, who is my greatest and deepest love." *Irena*

"We are a group of five sister-in-laws and friends that are very close. We laugh, we cry, and we take mini-vacations together. The most important memory for me was how my friends rallied around me when I went through my mother's illness and subsequent passing. They took care of my kids and my house. They brought food to the hospital, they prayed and cried with me, and helped me to accept and make the hardest decision of my life. Afterwards, they helped me go on and remember my mother in a positive way. Our group enjoys getting together, so we have what we call 'stress-reliever Fridays'. We talk about our kids and their problems or accomplishments, we talk about the men in our lives, we drink wine, and, if we are having a really good time, we might even sing karaoke! We are there for each other. As the time has passed, we have grown older and gone through hard times and good times together. We call ourselves "Las Comadres." This is the name in Spanish that you call someone who is the godparent of your child. We have all become godmothers of each other's kids. And, after all this time, we still have too much fun!" *Isabel*

The language of friendship
is not words, but meanings.

HENRY DAVID THOREAU

Always be kind, for everyone
is fighting a hard battle.

PLATO

Celebrate birthdays—always

The age doesn't matter, but remembering the day does!

Nurturing and Celebrating

*A friend is a present you
give yourself.*

ROBERT LOUIS STEVENSON

The importance of nurturing the connections with our girlfriends
cannot be taken lightly. Long-lasting ties with girlfriends can make,
and keep us healthier. This is not wishful thinking—it's backed up
by research and study. Those sweet moments spent chatting over

tea and biscuits are actually good for our health and well-being—
perhaps just as good as spending time in the gym.

While we all benefit from technology and the ability to stay connected
24/7, make an effort to talk face-to-face. Yes, texting is great, and email
and other social networking options are all terrific—they've opened up
a whole new world of options for us to stay in touch. However, try to
get upfront and personal every now and then. There's nothing like
physical contact to reinforce that closeness we crave.

Girlfriend get-togethers allow us to share deeper parts of ourselves.
The smiles, laughter, and the actual warmth of the hugs you'll receive
make it well worth the effort of carving out girlfriend time. Try to find
an excuse to have a girl's night out, to escape on a weekend yoga retreat,
or to meet for the occasional lunch. And if you can only manage phone
calls and emails, then do that. Just stay connected. Nurture and
celebrate one another, because it's all good.

"I had one of my greatest challenges during an upheaval in my life over fifteen years ago—a time when I really needed my friends' support, and this is what I discovered: True girlfriends are the ones who stand by you in your darkest hour. While others walk away, only a select few march toward you and become even closer friends. They are there through the good, the bad, and especially the ugly. They nurture you and love you, asking for nothing in return." *Barbara*

"Soul sister girlfriends mean the world to me. They listen to your every word and sincerely care about what you are saying. They never judge you no matter what you say or do, and they are always there for you, especially when you need them the most." *Vanna*

Reciprocate

Friendships, like gardens, need tender loving care and attention to grow.
With girlfriends, as in all relationships, this requires a subtle dance of give and take,
but not one of keeping score, or tit for tat. Enjoy what you receive, and then
enjoy giving back as well. Nurture and cultivate your friendships.

"I grew up as an older sister to a baby brother. We have an unbreakable bond that nothing can shatter, but I never realized how special a soul sister could be until I met my soon-to-be husband. He has a sister-in-law that I will be inheriting along with the rest of his wonderful family. She and I have a very special connection. We both grew up with only brothers and married into a family of all boys. I'd like to think that we each fill a sisterly void that we never knew we had. We laugh for hours, go on adventures and truly care about each other's well being. We now share the bond of family and, even though it's not blood, I love her as if it were. Family and 'sisters' (even in-laws) will be with you until the very end, if you're lucky. There is something extraordinary in realizing that even though you weren't born with a sister, you will inevitably find her, one way or another, along the way." *Jordyn*

Offer advice with compassion; accept advice with grace

We only truly know what we know about ourselves. Our opinions and recommendations are one perspective: our own. It's not up to us to be judge and jury—we're there to be honest, openhearted, and kind.

*Hold a true friend
with both hands.*

NIGERIAN PROVERB

Try to understand—even if you don't

Sometimes you just need
to be a sounding board.

"My girlfriend taught me it is okay to be human. With a girlfriend in your life, you can accept your imperfections and know you can set a new course for your life—one day at a time." *Suz*

"My girlfriends are like the perfect diamond—multifaceted, hard to find, difficult to give up, impossible to forget, and absolutely priceless. Couldn't live without them." *Lovey*

"The very best thing about girlfriends is that they offer you unconditional love. They never judge you and are always there to support you, both in good times and in bad." *Sherry*

"When I was a kid, my mom's favorite quote was 'The art of living is more like wrestling than dancing,' from the Greek emperor Marcus Aurelius. Girlfriends help your heart and soul sing, whether it's your time to wrestle or dance. They are there whether you need them or not. Girlfriends are like sisters without all the baggage." *Jeanne*

Forgive, forget, or move on

Holding a grudge is a waste of precious time. Everyone makes mistakes.
If you hold on to a grudge, you're the one who suffers from the anger and frustration.
Forgive and forget it, or move on. Friends are an important part of our lives—they
bring us joy, a sense of community, and, by having them in our lives, we can be
happier and healthier. They lift us up when we're down, they give us hugs when
we're sad, and they're our cheerleaders for the good times in our lives. Though it
may not be possible to maintain a close relationship with all the girls you meet, if you
really, truly cannot get along with someone, then at least withdraw your 'cat claws'
and be mature about it. Life is too short to hold on to anger. Nurture the good friends
you enjoy, and try to learn lessons from everyone who steps into your path.

Blessed is the influence of one true,
loving human soul on another.

GEORGE ELIOT

*It is one of the blessings of old friends that you
can afford to be stupid with them.*

RALPH WALDO EMERSON

"Girlfriends best be chosen wisely. Girlfriends need to be bountiful, not plentiful; protective secret-keepers who pull you up and sometimes back. They tell you the truth. They strongly tether you when your moorings are loose, and happily celebrate your flying. They love you. And you need to be a girlfriend back – it's a reciprocal relationship." *Gail*

"Our paths cross and souls connect through our adventures and dreams. We look at each other without judgment and understand the universe a little bit more—soul to soul, heart to heart." *Catherine*

*Only your real friends will tell you
when your face is dirty.*

SICILIAN PROVERB

41

"Emotional bonds with a girlfriend can navigate both time and space. You may live in different cities, perhaps even on different continents, but your friendship won't be shaken. I have a friendship like that. We've both found that a phone call, an email, or a hand-written letter can reach across the expanse and bring warmth and a deep abiding sentiment that resonates with pleasure for us both. Such a friendship is a treasure indeed…one to be cherished." *Cheryl*

A true friend is someone who knows there's something wrong even when you have the biggest smile on your face.

UNKNOWN

Reach out

If one of your friends is the hermit type, make an effort
to draw her out of her shell. A little encouragement
from a girlfriend may help to smooth some of life's
rough edges just when we need it the most.

*Nothing but heaven itself is better than
a friend who is really a friend.*

PLAUTUS

Comforting
and Tending

One good heart attracts another.
Each true friend deserves the other.

SHAKER SAYING

The special relationship of girlfriends is a phenomenon that we as women have long understood and relished, but that scientists have only recently begun to analyze in earnest. The reason being a simple, yet critical one—girlfriends are good for our health!

Yet, on top of this salient little tidbit, there is another, perhaps even more intriguing fact—maintaining and nurturing girlfriends may actually protect us against life-threatening illness. Now, that's something worth clucking about.

Whatever the specialists say, women the world over certainly know that having good girlfriends and cultivating relationships over time brings joy and goodwill into our lives. Make time for your girlfriends. Resist the urge to put them on the back-burner when your life gets overwhelming, and stressful, because—guess what? —that is precisely when you need your girlfriends the most. Put on the kettle or chill a bottle of wine, or grab your yoga mat, your surfboard, your jogging shoes, your knitting, your cookie dough, your meow mix, or whatever catnip you need to inspire you to rally round your girlfriends and just let your girlfriend-comfort time begin. And then repeat. Again and Again. See? Even the thought of your gal pals can make you smile.

Friends are angels who lift us to our feet when our wings have trouble remembering how to fly.

UNKNOWN

"Spiritual connections are conditional on our openness and readiness to accept them. I bonded with like-minded girls as a pre-teenager when we joined a group called *Habonim* (The Builders), to collect money for UNICEF. We found such joy in each other, no matter what our economic status or physical appearances. My own 'blood' sister, six years older than me, was always in a different place, and it took many years before we connected. As my mom grew older, and 'maturity' set in, I found that age differences didn't matter. We are now so close, and laugh, share, and cry together. I feel so lucky. I am still close to those girls from my teenage years. They are my life-long soul sisters. Plus, I have my 'blood' sister, who, to my great surprise, has become a soul sister too!" *Sue*

"About nineteen years ago, I had a serious cancer scare. The morning I was scheduled for surgery, one of my dearest girlfriends was the one who took me to the hospital to check me into the cancer center. Oddly, my husband who was usually so strong, had gotten a little freaked out about the whole thing, and had decided to skip the preliminaries, and come to the hospital just before I went into the operating room. I understood. My girlfriend and I would handle the fear and emotion of it all in a different way, as women do. I was scared but trying to be brave. The experience was truly a moment of reckoning for me. I never told my kids or my parents how serious it was. While I filled out forms and got prepped for my surgery, my girlfriend was by my side. She was a steady, loving force holding my hand, calming me, helping me find my inner courage. She kept me breathing in a regular pattern, and reminded me to focus on the positive outcome I was praying for. In the end, I was one of the lucky ones, and I am fine…cancer-free. This girlfriend is still one of my dearest, most steadfast girlfriends, and I will always be grateful for her strength and love during some of my darkest hours." *Charlyn*

Girlfriend Time

is good for your health, mentally
and physically. Do your best to
make time for it.

"Here's a great thought given to me by my dearest girlfriend: Where you are now is just fine." *Susie*

Everywhere, we learn only from those whom we love.

JOHANN VON GOETHE

"Soul sisters transcend time and space. Soon after I moved to the West Coast, I met a group of women who all became fast friends. Living it up in our twenties, we have many fond memories of adventures all across Southern California. One friend in particular has become one of my closest friends. We had our weddings within months of each other. We had our two children in the same years. Unfortunately, she relocated back to the Midwest to be closer to family. But this hasn't put a dent in our relationship. If anything, it has only grown stronger. She is the person I call when I am frustrated with life and need a listening ear. She is the person who calls when she has fabulous news about her kids, her career, or her husband. We can make each other laugh and cry in a matter of minutes. No distance will get in the way of our friendship and support of one another. I wish we were able to do weekly dinners and playdates, but we are certainly not going to let a little bit of a location issue interfere with our sisterhood. It is the presence of friends like this that make me a better person. Her words and counsel help put the little hiccups in life in perspective. We remind each other that our children are not out of the ordinary, that our relationships are not perfect, but still worth working on, that our careers are on the right track. We support each other in the good times and the bad. And we wish the best for one another—unconditional love that transcends time and space. I am very lucky." *Marni*

"Years ago, I was going through a particularly difficult period of my life, but was reluctant to share anything about it. I thought it was too personal—it concerned someone in my family, a child, who was dealing with a terrible illness—and though I trusted my girlfriends, I just didn't have the energy to reach out to them. I was consumed by sadness, and so I became a hermit. One day, I had gone to a hair salon, trying to keep up normal appearances by doing everyday things. Two of my best girlfriends simply showed up while I was sitting there, staring into space, numb, and despondent. They wrapped their arms around me, and I dissolved into tears—something I had desperately needed to do. They sat with me for hours, helping me cope, bringing me back to a place of strength and courage. My girlfriends are selfless, intuitive angels—they were my Rock of Gibraltar when I needed them to be." *Flora*

"I have a new friend who has become a best friend because she *is* the best friend. I was apparently sicker than I thought, and three times a day there was a call to my hospital bed with a little update from the exciting outside world and it brightened my days. Sunshine and surprises—a gift of a friend. I have learned to be a better friend—a more intuitive friend—more attentive to sharing moments and adventures." *Gail*

*The only way to have
a friend is to be one.*

RALPH WALDO EMERSON

Girlfriends show
up for each other

Be ready and willing to offer
a shoulder to cry on, and
a comforting hug.

Girlfriends are intuitive

They pick up on each other's emotional needs. Sometimes, just being present is enough.

Being deeply loved by someone gives you strength, while loving someone deeply gives you courage.

LAO-TZU

"The truest friend holds up a mirror inside our soul and sees the special spark that lives in our heart. I can trust her with all of me, knowing that the times I may not like what I see inside myself, she is always there to remind me that I am not alone. I will have her love to sustain me during the time that I find it hard to nourish myself. She is my rock, my laughter, the beauty in all things, hope and a safe haven that, in the changing reality of time, always remains constant and true. She is love." *Lili*

"When you are at breaking point, and you ask yourself, 'what do I need to consider for my life now?', a true girlfriend will toss out some fabulous suggestions—she might even make you laugh. Most certainly, she will help you know you can go on." *Susan*

Ah, how good it feels! The hand of an old friend.

HENRY WADSWORTH LONGFELLOW

"I had a dear girlfriend who stayed close despite weeks, or even months, without us seeing each other. Once, because of a temporary relocation, we even endured a year of separation, and then only communicated sporadically. Yet the special link between us remained almost sacrosanct. We got each other, like no one else could. When we did have the chance to get together in person, we were like giddy young girls—happy to see one another. We would pick up where we left off, as though we had never been apart. We gave each other advice, talked about our kids, the men in our lives, our careers—everything and anything. She's gone now, but I have memories that I will always cherish. The unique friendship we shared touched me deeply, and her essence will be wrapped around my heart for as long as I live." *Taylor*

Soul Sisters are safe

When you're with your girlfriend, you know you're
in a safe harbor, and you can be yourself.

And finally...

We've all heard the old proverb, 'Birds of a feather flock together.'
Well, girlfriends do this in spades. During our lives, we will gravitate
toward women with whom we can form a sense of community.
Whether we meet through our jobs, religious affiliations, families,
kids' schools, or partners, once we've made a connection that feels
good, we'll nurture and tend it, because we know we need it. If we're
lucky, some of those connections will turn into enduring bonds—soul
sister friendships that are strong enough to weather the storms of life.

These girlfriends are the ones who will comfort you during your
darkest hours—a battle with cancer, the illness of a child, the pain
of a divorce, the sorrow of the death of a loved one. They'll also be
there to soothe you through the less catastrophic but still unfortunate
ongoing daily vexations that are not life-threatening, but can still
nudge your cortisol levels into the stratosphere. They will
congratulate you when you become a mother, aunt, or grandmother,
and knit booties for the baby. These girlfriends will even understand
if you are so swamped that you have to beg off on your girl's night
out. But then they'll fill you in on the latest news, and quickly set up

another date so as not to leave you out. In other words, they care. That's a special kind of love. Doesn't it feel good to know you've got someone (or perhaps several someones) in your corner?

Please continue to be the good girlfriends and connected soul sisters you already are. You make a world of difference to your gal pals. Flock together as often as you can, lovely birds. Tweet away with abandon. Girlfriends are good for you, and you're all extremely beneficial for each other, bound together as you are, heart and soul. Savor these connections and treasure them. You are soul sisters!

I expect to pass through this world but once. Any good, therefore, that I can do, or any kindness that I can show to any fellow creature, let me do it now. Let me not defer or neglect it, for I shall not pass this way again.

ETIENNE DE GRELLET

Picture credits

Acknowledgments

With affection, I dedicate this book to my soul sisters.

Girlfriends have made the loveliest difference in my life. In essence, it is their uncanny ability to make me feel 'really good.' I humbly thank you all for giving me this gift. I shall always try my best to reciprocate.

At times in my life, girlfriends provided a different lens, helping me view a difficult situation in another way. Other times, they've offered a safe place to cry, complain, or flesh out new ideas. I can happily say that my girlfriends almost always make me feel good so, given the opportunity, we're simply content to be together.

I will always think of you all with fondness, and feel blessed to have the girlfriend relationships I've made over the years. Though some of you are gone, you'll *never* be forgotten. We'll always be soul sisters.

In loving memory of Stephanie and Nancy